For my father-in-law, Seung Hwan Cho, who showed
me Saturn for the first time through a telescope
in South Korea, and for our amazing Creator God.
—TC

To all those curious little minds who want
to know what lies beyond the stars.
—MAM

WRITTEN BY **Tina Cho**

ILLUSTRATED BY **Marta Álvarez Miguéns**

God's Little Astronomer

WATERBROOK

Little astronomer, let's take a trip to outer space, high above the mountains, clouds, and sky.

Out the window, you will see the wonders God has made.

Before the mountains were born,
before you gave birth to the earth and the world,
from beginning to end, you are God.

—Psalm 90:2

God created the galaxies. You live in the Milky Way.
This swirl of gas, dust, and billions of stars
floated through the universe when God spoke.

OUR SOLAR SYSTEM

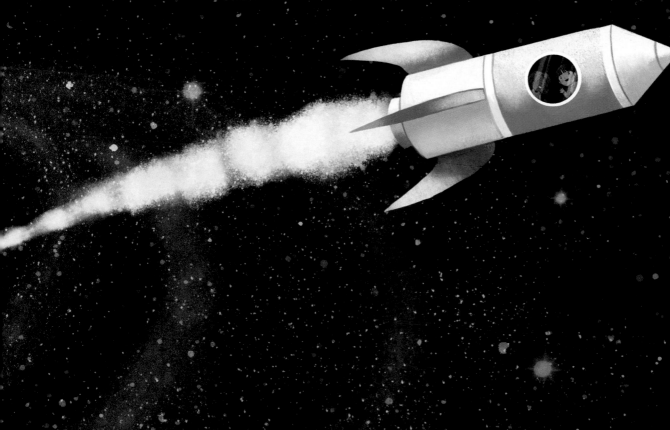

The Lord merely spoke,
*   and the heavens were created.*
He breathed the word,
*   and all the stars were born.*
*   —Psalm 33:6*

A galaxy is made up of gas,
dust, stars, and planets, which
are kept together by gravity.
There are more than 100 billion
galaxies in the universe. Earth is
part of the Milky Way galaxy.

Every star glows with heat and light. Some are giants. Some are dwarfs. Did you know—stars can be red, orange, yellow, white, or blue? Our Creator used a palette of colorful lights to paint the universe. Each star is a guide to **His goodness and love for you.**

White Dwarf Star

Orange Dwarf Star

Yellow Dwarf Star

Blue Giant Star

Red Giant Star

Red Supergiant Star

The sun has one kind of glory, while the moon and stars each have another kind. And even the stars differ from each other in their glory.
—1 Corinthians 15:41

Although we often draw stars with five points, they are balls of gas, made of hydrogen and helium. Stars look small from Earth, but that's because they are so far away. They also look white, but did you know stars are actually different colors? Astronomers can tell the temperature of a star based on its color: Blue stars are the hottest, followed by white and yellow. The cooler stars are orange and red.

There are more than 200 billion trillion stars, yet God counts them and knows their names. More amazingly, He knows *your* name and watches you **shine** in the world.

*He counts the stars
and calls them all by name.*
—Psalm 147:4

On a clear night, you might see 3,000 stars with your own eyes. With a telescope, you might see 100,000 stars. In our galaxy, there are more than 100 billion stars!

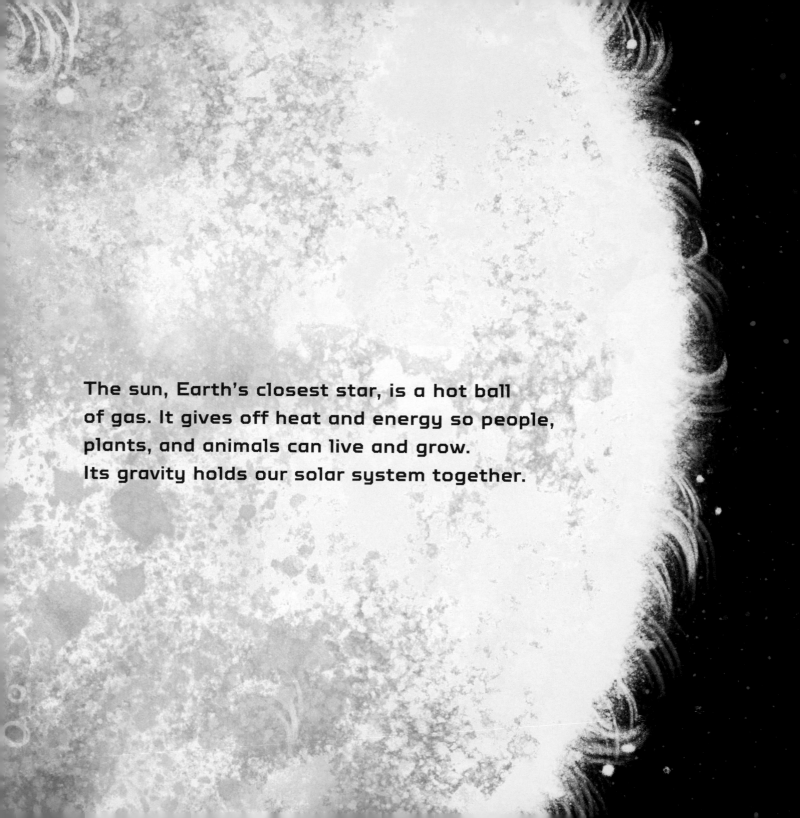

The sun, Earth's closest star, is a hot ball
of gas. It gives off heat and energy so people,
plants, and animals can live and grow.
Its gravity holds our solar system together.

*From the rising of the sun to the place where it sets,
the name of the LORD is to be praised.*
—Psalm 113:3, NIV

Our solar system is made up of the sun and everything that orbits, or circles, it. The sun is a middle-sized yellow star that is 27 million degrees Fahrenheit at its core, or center. The sun is 93 million miles away from Earth. If you drove a car 93 miles per hour, it would take 1 million hours to reach the sun—way more than 100 years!

Eight planets travel around the sun.
First the rocky planets: **Mercury, Venus, Earth, and Mars.**
Then giant planets of gas: **Jupiter, Saturn, Uranus, and Neptune.**
God set them in their places and keeps them in perfect order.
How great is our God!

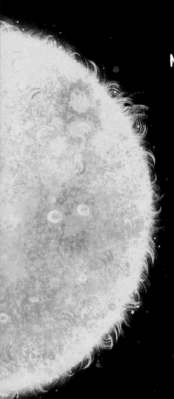

MERCURY

Because Mercury is so close to the sun, one orbit takes only 88 days. If you lived on Mercury, you'd have four birthdays in an Earth year.

EARTH

Earth, the third rocky planet, takes a little more than 365 days to orbit the sun. Every four years, the calendar has an extra day (February 29) to make up for the partial days.

VENUS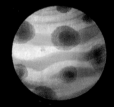

Venus is the hottest planet because of its thick atmosphere. It takes 225 days to orbit the sun.

MARS

Mars is called the Red Planet because of iron in the rocky ground. It takes 687 days to orbit the sun.

URANUS

JUPITER

Uranus is a blue-green color because of methane gas. This ice giant with thirteen rings spins on its side. If you lived on Uranus, you wouldn't have your first birthday until you were 84 Earth years old!

Jupiter, the biggest gas planet, has swirly clouds and a Great Red Spot storm. It orbits the sun in about 12 Earth years or 4,333 days.

God made the earth by his power.
He used his wisdom to build the world.
He used his understanding to stretch out the skies.
—Jeremiah 10:12, ICB

Don't miss the dwarf planets: Ceres, Pluto, Eris, Haumea, and Makemake. Though far away and small, they still matter to God—just like you.

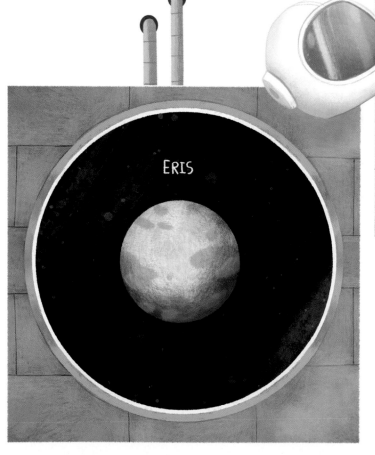

Dwarf planets are similar to planets because they orbit the sun and have a round shape. However, unlike planets, dwarf planets have other objects like asteroids sharing their orbital paths. The best-known dwarf planet is Pluto.

Through [Jesus] God created everything
in the heavenly realms and on earth.
He made the things we can see
and the things we can't see—
such as thrones, kingdoms, rulers, and authorities
in the unseen world.
Everything was created through him and for him.
—Colossians 1:16

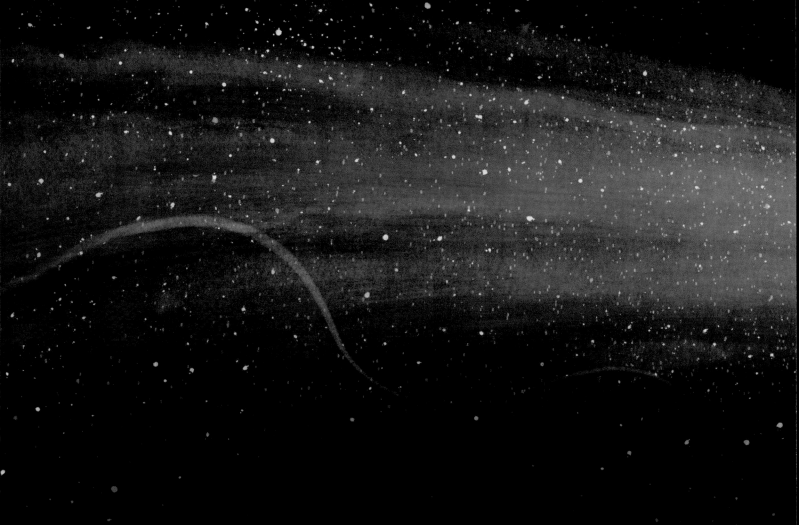

God made comets—giant snowballs that whiz
around the sun. From Earth, you might see
their long bright tails stream across the sky.
What an awesome display of God's power!

The breath of God makes ice.
And the wide waters become frozen.
—Job 37:10, ICB

A comet is a ball of ice, dust, and rock
that orbits the sun. Light and wind
from the sun form the comet's tail.

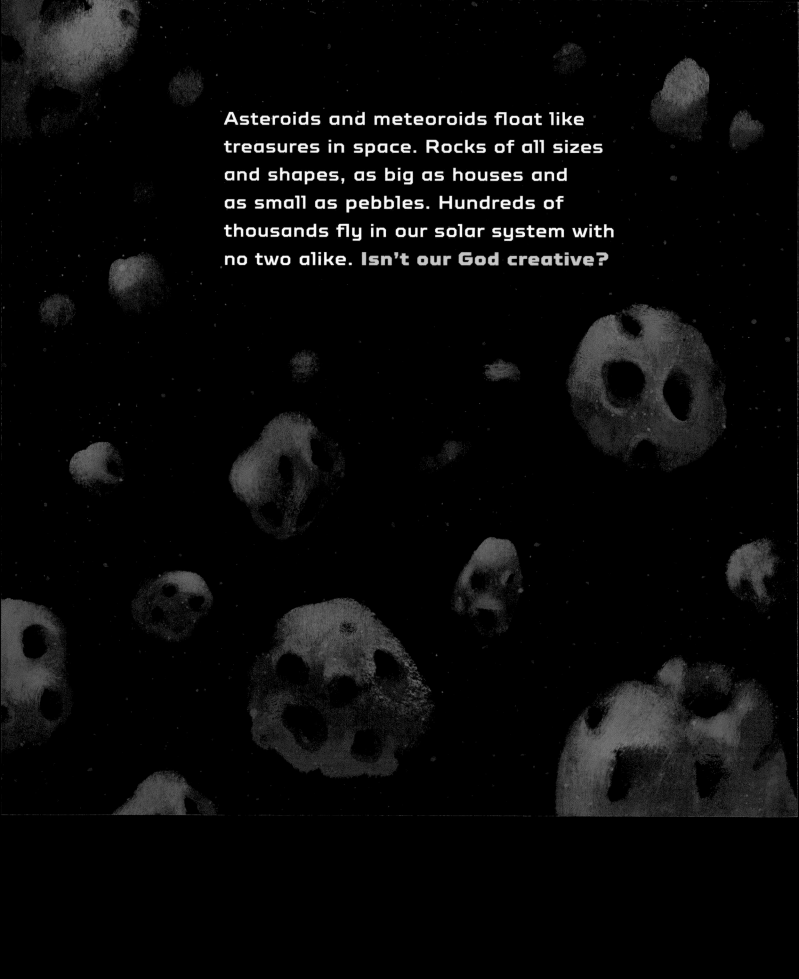

Asteroids and meteoroids float like
treasures in space. Rocks of all sizes
and shapes, as big as houses and
as small as pebbles. Hundreds of
thousands fly in our solar system with
no two alike. **Isn't our God creative?**

Asteroids are big rocks made of smaller rocks, clay, and metal. Asteroids can be metallic or stony. Many asteroids are found between Mars and Jupiter. Meteoroids are small rocks or pieces of metal in space. They fall or chip off asteroids, comets, planets, and even the moon.

You are worthy, O Lord our God,
to receive glory and honor and power.
For you created all things,
and they exist because you created what you pleased.
—Revelation 4:11

Let's zoom in on home—our planet Earth!
Swirling clouds above oceans, mountains, jungles,
deserts, and plains. So much for you to explore.
Wherever you go, God watches over you.

The earth is the Lᴏʀᴅ's, and everything in it.
The world and all its people belong to him.
—Psalm 24:1

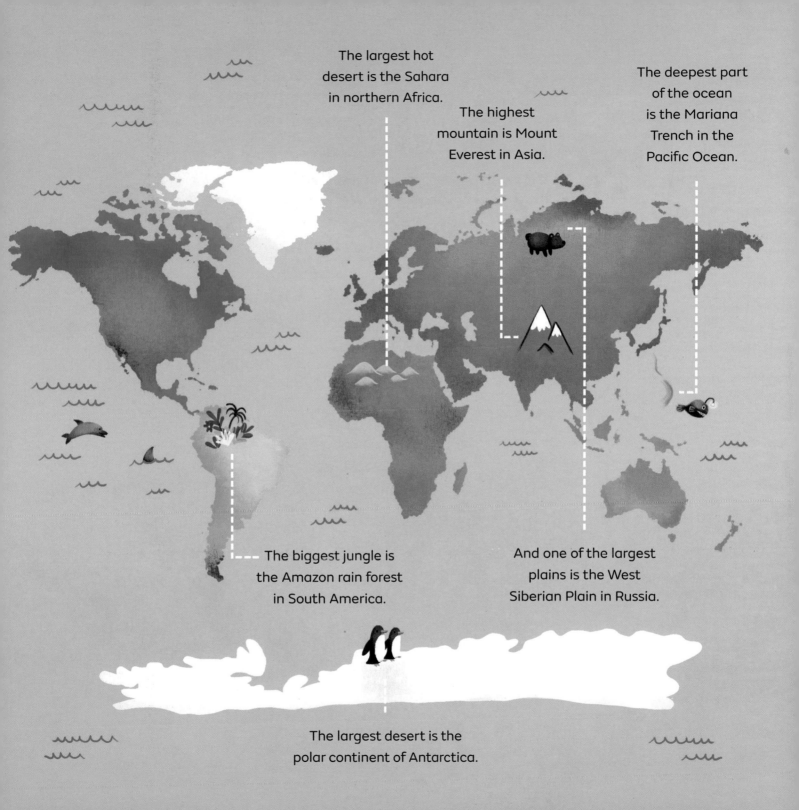

The largest hot desert is the Sahara in northern Africa.

The highest mountain is Mount Everest in Asia.

The deepest part of the ocean is the Mariana Trench in the Pacific Ocean.

The biggest jungle is the Amazon rain forest in South America.

And one of the largest plains is the West Siberian Plain in Russia.

The largest desert is the polar continent of Antarctica.

Earth is filled with everything you need: air to breathe, water to drink, and food to eat. God created the animals and plants, but humans, like *you*, are His ultimate creation. You will do marvelous things here!

Earth has the right amount of oxygen for humans, animals, and plants to breathe. God placed Earth the perfect distance from the sun. It's not too hot and not too cold. No other planet in our solar system is made perfectly for you!

The LORD is God,
and he created the heavens and earth
and put everything in place.
He made the world to be lived in.
—Isaiah 45:18

All day and night, Earth spins as it travels around the sun.
Each year, you complete one orbit on this unique planet.
As you circle the gigantic universe and continue to grow,
know that **God cares for you**—wherever His path leads you.

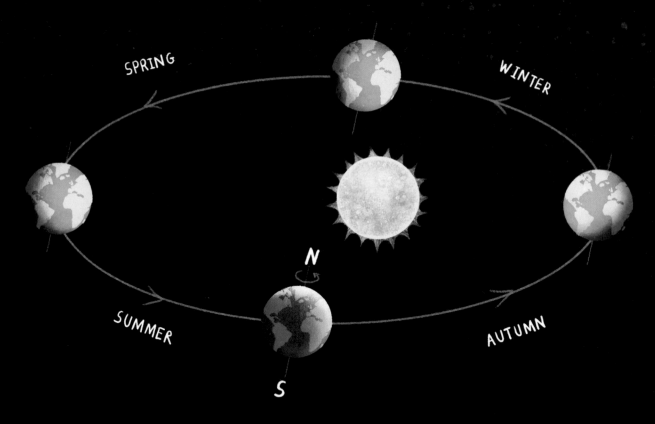

*You placed the world on its foundation
so it would never be moved.*
—Psalm 104:5

Earth completes one spin in twenty-four hours. When your side of Earth faces the sun, this is your day. When your side of Earth faces away from the sun, this is your night. On your birthday, you could celebrate a year of traveling around the sun!

what star pictures do you see
that point to Creator God?

SCORPIUS

CANIS MAJOR

CYGNUS

DRACO

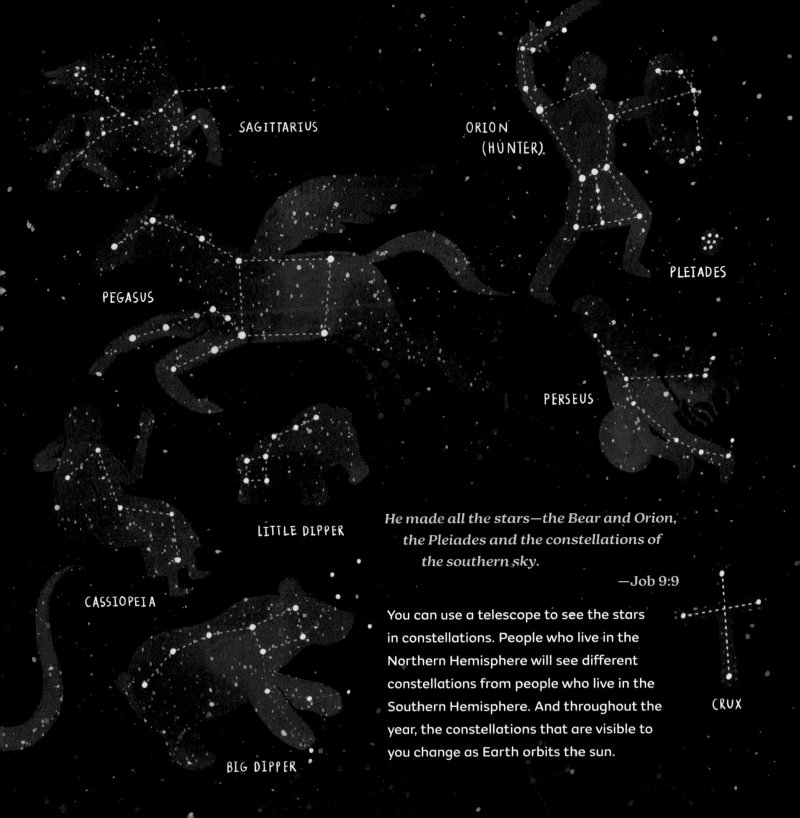

SAGITTARIUS

ORION
(HUNTER)

PEGASUS

PLEIADES

PERSEUS

LITTLE DIPPER

He made all the stars—the Bear and Orion,
the Pleiades and the constellations of
the southern sky.

—Job 9:9

CASSIOPEIA

You can use a telescope to see the stars
in constellations. People who live in the
Northern Hemisphere will see different
constellations from people who live in the
Southern Hemisphere. And throughout the
year, the constellations that are visible to
you change as Earth orbits the sun.

CRUX

BIG DIPPER

Remember the rocky meteoroids?
Sometimes they fall into Earth's sky,
becoming meteors, burning up as they
streak through the atmosphere. Have
you ever seen "shooting stars" zoom by?

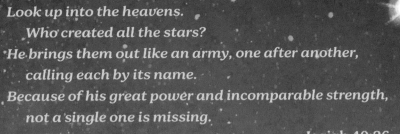

Look up into the heavens.
  Who created all the stars?
He brings them out like an army, one after another,
  calling each by its name.
Because of his great power and incomparable strength,
  not a single one is missing.

                                    —Isaiah 40:26

Rocky pieces that break off asteroids are called meteoroids. When they fall into Earth's atmosphere, they are called meteors. Meteors that don't burn all the way up are called meteorites when they hit the ground. When lots of meteors fall in one spot, it's called a meteor shower.

Look up at the moon, your closest neighbor in space, a giant nightlight. Watch the moon as it changes from phase to phase. From new moon to crescent to first quarter to waxing gibbous to full, each phase is created by sunlight shining on the moon's surface.

He made the moon to mark the seasons,
and the sun knows when to go down.
—Psalm 104:19, NIV

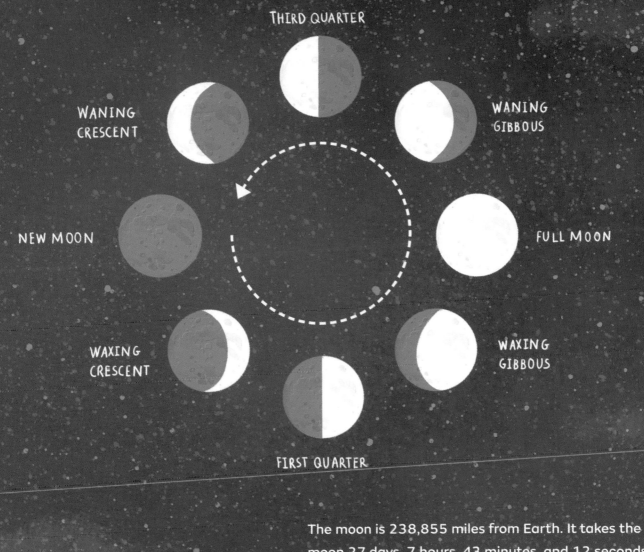

THIRD QUARTER

WANING GIBBOUS

WANING CRESCENT

FULL MOON

NEW MOON

WAXING CRESCENT

WAXING GIBBOUS

FIRST QUARTER

The moon is 238,855 miles from Earth. It takes the moon 27 days, 7 hours, 43 minutes, and 12 seconds to travel around Earth. Although it looks like it, the moon doesn't change sizes. In fact, the sun always shines on half the moon. But because the moon orbits Earth, and Earth orbits the sun, we see different amounts of the light shining on the moon.

Sun, moon, and stars beam from afar, displaying **God's wondrous love**. Little astronomer, know that our Father in heaven, our cool Creator, sees *you* as His most special creation in all the universe.

Our heavenly Father expertly designed the universe. The same God who created the massive planets, sun, stars, and moon made you. Thank Him for creating this incredible world for you to enjoy. God displays His goodness and love for you in His extravagant creation.

When I look at the night sky and see the work of your fingers—
the moon and the stars you set in place—
what are mere mortals that you should think about them,
human beings that you should care for them?

—Psalm 8:3–4